Listen to the Quiet

written by
Helen DePuydt

ISBN: 9798723656529
Imprint: Independently published

The author has retold events, locales from her experiences and recorded conversations with the Kientz Family.

Listen To The Quiet
Poem by Luella M. (Kientz) Lofthus

An eagle soars high, in the sky,
While fluffy white clouds go floating by.

A butterfly rests on a wet leaf after a shower
While bumble bees spread pollen from flower to flower.

The robins listen for a worm in the grass,
And a flock of geese honk overhead as they pass.

The spider is busy spinning his lacy web,
And the ant mounds up dirt for the rains ahead.

The weathervane rooster points to the north,
A balmy breeze swings him, back and forth.

All of God's creatures have a song to sing,
Birds chirp and warble and the squirrels chatter about everything.

Old Glory waves from the post by the porch,
Our thanks to the many who carried the torch.

If you want to relax and have peace for a bit
Tune into nature and listen to the quiet.

Introduction

Traveling from an urban setting back to my childhood home on the family farm in NE Montana, I become immediately aware of how quiet it is in the Big Sky Country. With no internet or cell phone service at my mother's house, it is the perfect writer's retreat where my mother and I can *Listen To The Quiet* and compile this book; the origins of which began back in 1973.

Although I was only 3 years old in '73, I remember well the visits to our neighbors, the Kientzes, who lived approximately 5-6 miles away. While my older siblings were at school, I would accompany my mother to the original 1919 homestead home where the Keintz family lived quite comfortably without modern amenities such as electricity and plumbing. There was no hum of electrical appliances or buzz of overhead power lines at the Kientz home. My mother was fascinated that this family still did EVERYTHING the "old way". I particularly remember the delicious corn chowder Leona Kientz would prepare on the old time wood stove.

While my mother visited with Leona and her parents Otto and Lizzie Keintz, I occupied myself easily and quietly so the adults could visit. I would gaze with admiration at the diamond willow wood creations carved and polished by Otto. I was not allowed to touch these curvaceous pieces of functional art for they were commissioned in advance from other admirers across the country.

We visited primarily during the spring and summer, however, my solo playtime was limited to the indoors. I was sternly told that I was not allowed to stray outside or go to the outdoor privy unaccompanied due to potential danger of snakes and coyotes.

Believing their homesteading adventures would make an interesting lifestyle story for modern readers of the time, my mother suggested the idea to Zane Tollefson, the editor of the local news publication. Zane agreed that the Kientz story should indeed be written and printed in the publication. As my mother remembers it, "he twisted her arm" to be the one to write the story.

I believe to this day that my mother probably didn't need that much convincing as she already visited the neighbors regularly and had a personal love of writing. So off we would go, mother and youngest child, to hear the remarkable tales of these Montana homesteaders.

My mother took notes during their conversations and on occasion used a battery powered tape recorder. She would then return home and would somehow manage to find the time between caring for her large family to write one chapter a week for publication in the Independent Tribune.

I have compiled and adapted the articles my mother wrote back in the 70s inside this book in dedication to my mother, the author, on her 90th birthday.

Theresa (DePuydt) Johnson

Contents

Part 1

1973

You will find as you leave the country road and turn onto the winding prairie trail, you are leaving the noisy distractions of modern life behind. The tall toothpick-like sentinels bringing electricity and phone service to the widespread ranches and farms, do not turn into this rustic home on the knoll, a mile to the west. This is entirely by choice, not necessity.

Visualize, if you will, an east window framed prettily by flowering plants with the early morning sunlight filtering through the lacy leaves of the Virginia creeper growing majestically against the outside of the house. The view of the horizon is the rugged Frenchman breaks; the choice hunting grounds for countless deer hunters each autumn. Winding like a narrow gray ribbon a mile away, the Frenchman Creek Road seemingly slices the prairie in half from north to south.

Those sunbeams fall and ricochet off the shiny linoleum floor of the small combination dining-living room. Let your eyes wander for a few minutes over the stunning miniature-flowering orchid plants, the petrified carrot lying among other curiosities on the window shelf. If you are 6-feet tall, you will have to duck to avoid bumping into a small hand-carved replica of Lindbergh's famous plane, 'The Spirit of St. Louis', dangling from the ceiling above the window. The creation was not an exact replica however as it was two-winged while Lindbergh's plane was monoplane. The walls of this room and the bedroom on the south are lined with a wide assortment of memorabilia, mostly handmade long ago by some member of the Kientz family.

Nearly everything in this house has a fascinating history. Take for example, the hydrangea plant with the showy blossoms. This plant is an offspring of the original plant which traveled to Montana via the railroad in 1913, when the Kientz family moved here from Blue Earth, Minnesota. That shiny linoleum is the same one which was placed on the floor in 1920, and which had been ordered from M. W. Savage, mail-order house in Minneapolis and brought by horse-drawn sled from Saco, Montana, the nearest town, a distance of 23 miles. That trip was not without mishap. The 12-foot wide linoleum (not inlaid) tipped off the sled into the deep snow, but was unharmed. If you want the secret of its longevity, it's the loving care given it each year – a coat of varnish applied in the morning and the linoleum is ready for use by evening. The result after these many years is a mellowed appearance very similar to decoupage.

Now, let us meet the occupants of the country home, for they have aroused the curiosity of visitors for some time. Curiosity is the proper word because by far and large, many individuals believe that happiness and expensive worldly goods are synonymous; here is a family which can dispel that line of thinking. The two ladies of this tiny rustic home are Lizzie Kientz, 86 years of age and her blonde daughter, Leona. Lizzie is a replica of Whistler's Mother, ruffled cap atop the silvery hair and slender hands folded on her lap. Don't let her frail appearance fool you – those hands were extremely busy hands as you will soon discover. The lone man of the household is Otto, who is quick to tell you – 87 years young. He is a craftsman, whittling on some item nearly every day. Otto, besides being a farmer-stockman, fisherman, mechanic and fiddler, is a man of many talents. Otto's playful wit sets the mood of this delightful home and which brings friends and relatives from far and wide. This alone is proof of the esteem this family enjoys in the community.

Leona, the eldest of the two daughters born to Lizzie and Otto, has been the mainstay of the family since the illness of her mother in February, 1958. She willingly relinquished a job on the west coast to return to the farm to care for her ailing mother and has been there ever since. Relaxing in the comfortable, cushioned rocker alongside the east window, one can't help but comment that Leona's choice was a wise one, noticing the sparkle of pride in her parents' eyes.

Besides the care of her invalid mother and household chores, Leona milks a cow which means butter to churn and cottage cheese to process at times. Raising chickens and caring for a few head of cows also are on her agenda. Besides this, the family is involved in rug weaving. This operation will be described later.

A bountiful garden is raised each year, which is watered by rainfall, supplemented by irrigation from a small reservoir to the south. The vegetable plants, such as tomatoes and Copenhagen cabbage, are started early in the house and set out after danger of frost. The Kientz garden is undoubtedly the earliest in the community. Although lacking modern conveniences, Leona considers her many responsibilities a labor of love.

Leona's younger sister, Luella "Babe," is Mrs. Arnold Loftos of Bremerton, WA, who has been employed for 28 years with Mountain Bell in Seattle. She is staff manager, which means much traveling, but this does not prevent her from finding time to visit frequently with her beloved family out here on the prairie of Montana.

Part 2

Some young men's thoughts turn to love in the spring, but for Otto Kientz, during this period of his life, his thoughts centered on the "Land of Opportunity," which was the vast prairie land of Montana. It was none too soon, as three years before[1], this territory was thrown open to homesteading and the days of the once-open range were quickly drawing to a close.

Anyway you look at it, this planned adventure, from Minnesota to Montana, took the courage of rugged individuals. The succeeding years proved this definitely was the "survival of the fittest."

There were no brass bands welcoming the young Minnesotan to the tiny town of Saco. The train passengers were dusty and tired, but this didn't seem to dampen their spirits.

---

1   Congress passed Enlarged Homesteading act of 1909

Quoting Mr. Kientz, "It was a beautiful day in Saco when I alighted from the 'skidoo', the local passenger train of those days. I had met two other men traveling on the train who were also bound for Montana. Tom Juelson, whose brother, Juel Juelson, was already settled in the area, and Charles 'Holledge' Allen from North Dakota." Juelson convinced his traveling companions that they should at least stop at Saco and look over the surrounding territory, which was available to the homesteaders. "Although my original destination had been Billings, I have no regrets to this day," claims Otto.

This was May 1913 – days not too many remember. As Lizzie Kientz remarks, "We are the only complete family among the original circle of neighbors; the rest are gone." - but the memories remain and what golden memories these are for the Kientz family.

Childhood friends Lizzie Prechel and Otto Kientz, both from solid German families of Blue Earth, Minnesota, were married June 20, 1912. Lizzie, the only girl among three brothers, had attended a German Lutheran School, as did Otto. The Preschels lived a mile from the Kientz family, although by road it was more like 7 miles. So, according to Kientz, "I didn't see Lizzie as often as I would have liked." Otto, whose family was larger, was third in a family of four boys and six girls.

The three young men, Juelson, Kientz and Allen, hired a livery team for the total price of $6 to take them north so they could scout over the country. Tom Juelson's brother, who as mentioned before was already settled, was most willing to show three prospective neighbors over the virgin land north of the Milk River. This was the Milk River that was so named by Lewis and Clark years before.

They first stopped at the A. J. Erickson homestead to get acquainted. This was about 20 miles from Saco. A. J. was the father of Ernest Erickson, retired farmer-rancher now living in the town of Saco.

Another person, an area resident by the unlikely name of Rattlesnake Olson also escorted the newcomers over the available land. Kientz eventually selected land adjoining the Erickson's on the east and Allen filed later on land north of Kientz.

When asked their reason for venturing out to this unknown territory, Otto remarked, "We rented a section of land after we were married, but it was extremely difficult to make a living – milking seven to 10 cows twice a day besides the farming. The Minnesota farm life also required hired help, so we decided after much soul-searching that I should take time to venture west to Montana and just see if Uncle Sam's homestead offer was worthwhile."

Moisture was plentiful that year with Rattlesnake Coulee north of Kientz's running and the winter before had been extremely mild, according to local residents. The future looked very encouraging, so after selecting their land sites, Charles Allen and Otto Kientz started walking south toward Saco. They walked as far as the Milk River Bridge. This was a high bridge a short distance west of the present Milk River Bridge. At this bridge, the two men were picked up by A. J. Erickson with his wagon and rode the remaining distance into Saco. This was a lucky break for them as the two were quite footsore by that time, as Otto recalls.

Although W. D. Miller was the U.S. Land commissioner stationed at Saco, the two tired men decided they would catch the skidoo back to Glasgow and file on their selected land with Otto Christiansen, land commissioner residing in that town.

While they were loafing at the Saco depot, one of the local men hanging around advised Kientz with the words, "You'll never be sorry for settling here – it's a healthy climate and the people are healthy, too."

Just at that moment, a skinny man, carrying a bottle of milk under his arm, came into view. Otto gestured toward him, saying, "Well, look at that fellow, he doesn't look so healthy!" The local resident replied, "Oh him, he's our local doctor and he's starving to death!" That doctor was the beloved Dr. R. V. Minnick. Apparently the Saco sage was correct about the local health, because according to Kientz, the local cemetery wasn't started until a man was shot in town.

The two filed on their land, which was located on a map and paid a fee of $23. Otto says he paid this with a check which "didn't even bounce." So now Charles Allen and Otto Kientz became official homesteaders in the so-called "wild west."

That night was to be spent in Glasgow, MT at the Shannon Hotel, but plans changed before sunrise – the two young men decided they couldn't spend any more time in bed, so they hopped a train back east to their homes. Some time later, the Shannon Hotel's bill caught up to them.

All the necessary arrangements were made for the Kientzes to move to their land awaiting them in Saco, Montana. The young couple's belongings were loaded into an immigrant car on the railroad. Lizzie's brother, Walt Preschel, agreed to ride in the car so he could care for the livestock, consisting of one dog and "no cats," Otto emphasized, along with four workhorses, 40 brown Leghorn chickens and one shorthorn milk cow. All the machinery and household furniture, including a high cupboard, which incidentally had glass doors and a Minnesota sewing machine. It must be mentioned that the Bucks cast iron cook stove and the previously mentioned household items are still in good use! The coal and wood stove was bought by Otto in 1908 and were 15 years old at the time of their move. This was used by Otto before he was married while one of his sisters kept house for him during his bachelor days. Lizzie, Otto's wife, never bought a loaf of bread in her life, it was all baked on this shiny black iron stove.

On September 23, 1913, Lizzie and Otto Kientz arrived with their possessions at the little Saco depot. The cost of transporting all their belongings amounted to $111. Oats had been poured over the machinery to conserve precious space. This feed was needed for the livestock and also for seed for future planting on the homestead. Everything reached Saco in good shape, even the glass-doored cupboard, which occupies the northeast corner of the Kientz's living room to this day. All these possessions were unloaded at the stockyards which was then located where the east grain elevator stands at Saco today. The machinery was transferred to Stile's livery barn, where the Krotsch house now is located at Saco.

The first year was an exceptionally busy year for this new family, while Lizzie stayed with the Ericksons, Otto and his brother-in-law made daily trips to Saco for lumber. They each drove a team, going into town one day and then bringing a load of building material back north the next. Byron & Nelson and Joe Rosendahl supplied the lumber at the modest price of less than $300. Otto reports that a total of 16 trips were made for lumber. "Within a week, a barn 16' x 36' was built," remarked Otto proudly, "the horses staying at one end and a floor was laid in the other part, which provided temporary living quarters for us until a house was built."

An unforgettable sight in those pre-barbed wire days to the people living in the barn, was an immense herd of sheep, divided by the building standing in their route; possibly 4,000 to 5,000 head estimated Otto, which were being herded by sheepherders to the Sweetgrass Hills. One of the sheepherders told Otto that if he could catch a sheep, he could keep it, but no such luck, as the sheep were just too fast. The sheepherder then set his dog on one sheep blind in one eye, and presented that to Otto. This sheep became a family pet, along with a few others given the couple by various neighbors.

Otto mentioned that while this building was going on, two female horseback riders, Mrs. Jansey Tieden and her sister, Clara, stopped to observe the activity.

Sometime later, Mrs. Tieden remarked that she had felt at that time that these unfortunate people wouldn't last very long out here on the prairie." The Tieden homestead was north and west of where the Kientzes were settling.

The next project on the agenda was the house building. It was decided that a small knoll to the west and a little to the south of the barn would be an ideal location.

First a cellar was dug with pick and shovel. According to Leona, "The dirt was so hard that the pick marks are still visible on the cellar walls!" The cellar proved to be an ideal cooler.

The shell of the house was built and the remaining lumber stored in one end. It must be mentioned that Lizzie was an able assistant to the men, helping to lift the boards into their proper positions and doing other odd jobs. By the 22nd of November, 1913, the family moved into the house from the barn. Much of the work was done at night by the flickering lights of kerosene lamps. One amusing incident which brings a twinkle to Otto's eye when he tells it, concerns the building of the south partition. After retiring for the night, it occurred to him that things weren't exactly as they should be, so he remarked to his wife, "Lizzie, I believe that I built that doorway wrong, the opening goes clear to the ceiling!" This error was rectified the following day, when Otto boxed in the upper part of the bedroom doorway.

Part 3

One philosophy of the homesteaders was, "Don't buy it if you can make do with a satisfactory substitute." Resourcefulness became second nature to these Montana settlers, and the Kientz family was no exception to the rule. For example, a nearby pit of sand became the source of their house insulation. It proved to be an excellent insulating material for their modest home, keeping it cool during torrid summer days and helping to warm it against the sub-zero winter temperatures prevalent in northern Montana.

Lizzie's job came next; painting the interior of the house. The walls had been covered with building paper. This durable material remains to this day, hidden by many layers of paint, accumulated over the years.

In 1913, the Kientz's first year in Montana, another task was high on the priority list of improvements – that was the making of a fireguard. Only the year before, fire had swept the land from the Milk River to the Canadian border. Part of the land occupied now by the Kientzes was included. The fire was fed by the lush grass and was unhampered by plowed fields, as widespread cultivation came in later years. Fire was probably more feared during the early 1900s than it is now, because of the scarcity of water and the lack of motorized vehicles; nor did these people have telephone service to enable them to warn others and call for assistance.

Getting back to the house once again, the stepping stones in front of this door are the same slab rocks brought from Rattlesnake Coulee in 1913. The original brick chimney is still being used and has never needed repairs, although the roof was redone once, three years ago. Other buildings cropped up to make the homestead more complete; the sod chicken coop – the sod having been plowed from the prairie. It hasn't been mentioned before but the primary building constructed by any homesteader is the little shack in the back. Some years later an ice house was constructed, which consisted of logs and dirt covering a pit. The large chunks of ice were cut during the winter at Otto's reservoir and then stored in straw and prairie grass to prevent melting. Otto says, "People even came from Whitewater to obtain ice for the making of ice cream."

There were other tasks to complete before winter set in. And important tasks they were, as the very lives of the homesteaders depended on fuel and water, and prevailing feed for their livestock.

Luckily Otto had brought along his sawing equipment to Montana. The 2-horse engine, weighing 500 pounds, operating a buzz-saw and powered by gasoline, certainly saved time in the actual sawing of the wood. Ash was the preferred wood for fuel since it burned more slowly in a heating stove. The wood in Rattlesnake Coulee was inaccessible with a wagon, so a team of horses was used for transporting the firewood from its source. This particular community of settlers was a bit more fortunate than some a few miles away to the west, who had no available timber for fuel and so, had to resort to the gathering up of the cow chips which was generally the job of the youngsters in the family.

The weight of Otto's bulky engine was 500 pounds, as mentioned previously. Compare this to a present day 2 hp engine, which can be carried in one hand! And by now, you have guessed it, that very same engine is still in use – pumping water!

Rattlesnake Coulee, source of so many essential items, provided water for the Kientzes during those first years. The four horses were driven down and were allowed to drink their fill at the flowing spring. Only then was water taken for house use and also for livestock.

This family was well supplied with canned goods taken from their Minnesota garden – even a jar of sauerkraut survived the long journey to Montana. The staples needed were purchased from the Saco stores: C.P. Martin, Bryon & Nelson and Harry Vagg. Bacon was one of the most desirable items, so much so, that it came to Saco by rail, in carload lots. Leona or "Toots," as she is affectionately known, commented that the family still has stone butter jars with the name HARRY VAGG imprinted on the sides. Other names around Saco may ring a bell with many longtime residents – I.C. Smith, depot agent; Charles Hess, local blacksmith and father of Mrs. Ernest "Maud" Erickson, was also a homesteader and neighbor of the Kientzes. The Erickson family now lives on the original Hess homestead.

The prairie grass was put up for hay late that first year. It proved to be abundant – this native grass was noted for its high nutritive value.

Otto mentioned that, "Our first winter spent in Montana proved to be mild, similar to this last winter (1972-73), although we had more snow during 1913-14." Little did they know that they wouldn't see their home state of Minnesota again, until 1926 – a span of 13 years.

The Valleytown post office was 3 miles to the east and that distance was faithfully walked by some member of the family three or four times a week. The name, post office, might be considered a blanket term, as it actually consisted of a store, bar and post office – not necessarily listed in order of importance. Mrs. Whitbread was postmistress and her husband managed the other two enterprises. The Whitbreads were originally from England. The two Whitbreads were weekly visitors at the Kientz home. Mrs. Whitbread died in 1942 and the post office was turned over to Allen Marshall to operate for the remaining years until mail service was initiated from Saco to this area north. After his wife's death, Mr. Whitbread took up tending bar for Sief Soennichsen at the Whitewater community. In 1945, Mr. Whitbread also passed away.

A false impression may be derived from listening to tales of hardship facing these settlers, so let us say that all was not work – time was taken out for various parties and dancing. Some in private homes, such as the Jansey Tieden home situated on Turkey Track, where people from all around helped them celebrate an anniversary that first year. One gentleman by the name of Mikkelson played a banjo and a lively time was had by all. This was reported by Otto Kientz, who didn't miss a party if he could help it.

The Tollefson School to the north was a frequent site for neighborhood dances. One in particular stays in the memory of the Kientzes. Some of the people remembered as being present, after all these years, were: Torgersons, Ericksons, Annie Eklund Hybeck, Hjelmer Reitan, Art Eklund, John Eklund and Cecil Hess. Cecil was a brother of Maud Erickson. Unknown to Cecil, his pet pig followed him north to the school house, obviously sensing some excitement. Sometime during the evening, a group of ladies ventured out in the dark to the outhouse but were unable to enter due to something or somebody forcing the door to remain closed. Needless to say, this caused quite a commotion that night. The next afternoon, Otto Kientz noted a small movement in the pasture to the north – sure enough, it was Cecil Hess's pet pig coming home from the schoolhouse, or shall we say the dance. The puzzle of the 'culprit in the outhouse' was solved.

"Toot's" and "Babe's" education was completed at the Tollefson Schoolhouse. During the winter months when weather was bad, their dad took them by sled to the schoolhouse and back. Their attendance was excellent. Lunches were packed daily in tobacco cans, which served as lunch pails. Mother Kientz found it necessary to bake bread frequently for the many sandwiches needed. Some tutoring was done at home, so by the time the two girls were of school age, they were very well prepared.

Anna Poland, the girls' first teacher, boarded with Kientzes as did another teacher, Luella "Tillie" McGears. During these years, courting was done in the Kientzes' living room – the unmarried schoolmarms proved quite popular with the neighborhood bachelors. Otto maintains that "this is a story all its own!" But, after some thought, it was decided that this would be passed over – at least for the time being.

Although the deer and the antelope still play, and God's paintbrush still paints a never-ending variety of sunsets, a gentle light has gone out in the Frenchman Creek Community and in the home of the Otto Kientz family. Mrs. Otto "Lizzie" Kientz, 86 years young, passed to her reward Friday evening. Gone, but certainly not forgotten, by those who knew her. Lizzie was a Christian lady in every way. She lived among the people she dearly loved and who took such tender care of her during her failing years. Lizzie was truly blessed with cheerfulness and her mind was good to the last. She was surrounded in her home by cherished belongings – such as her grandmother's handmade, appliqued quilt which covered her bed; and the prolific Virginia Creeper outside her window, which was started from a slip of vine she had purchased so many years ago. "The best 25¢ I ever spent," Lizzie had often said. These familiar things were precious to her and she was happy … her spirit was willing, but the body wasn't able.

Part 4

Religion played an important part in the community life of the homesteaders. The Kientzes belonged to the Lutheran congregation, which met once monthly at the Gus Pehlke home, beginning in 1916. Members would take turns meeting Pastor A. Jordan at Saco, where he arrived by skidoo. Pastor Jordon was stationed at Chinook, Montana and was single at this time. He was silent about possible romantic attachments and his congregation might have been in the dark to this day if it hadn't been for Mark Wright's sheepherder's weekly Chinook newspaper. One Sunday, Otto inquired about the Pastor's recent "life contract" and being a Christian. Pastor Jordon had to admit that he had taken a wife during his month's absence. The Chinook newspaper heading read, SIGNS LIFE CONTRACT.

Dinner was served to all attending the services in the Pehlke home and on one particular Sunday, with various denominations present, the overflowing table was upset by children playing underneath – food flew in all directions. This was a real crisis, because food preparation in those days was quite lengthy and the neighborhood grocery was many miles away. Somehow the ladies managed to scrape up enough "vittles" to satisfy everyone. Perhaps it was a small miracle, of the loaves and fishes variety. Anyway, as Otto described the event, it was a wonder how the ladies salvaged enough for a dinner.

In later years, this Lutheran congregation divided into two groups. The west community centralizing in the tiny hamlet of Whitewater and the remaining members organizing east, with services for awhile in the New Deal Schoolhouse. The east congregation, which the Kientzes belonged to, eventually bought the Corwin Center store and had it moved close to the Lars Solheim farm. This is another sign of the times along with vacant country schools and farm houses deteriorating after the families move into town. This little country church was the site of various church services and also fall dinners attended by people coming from far and wide. Politicians were quite noticeable during election years, enjoying the generous home-cooked meals and buying the handcrafts which were auctioned off during the evening. Wedding receptions and anniversary parties were also held in the little basement beneath the church. The Lutheran families in this community now travel into Saco for their church services.

Kientzes planted their first Montana garden in the spring of 1914, with "the good Lord watering it." These gardens provided the family with much needed fresh vegetables and enough surplus for Lizzie to can for the winter months.

1916 proved to be a year that the Frenchman Creek settlers won't forget. One March day, a letter arrived from Blue Earth, Minnesota, stating that Lizzie's parents were starting out for Montana on March 1st, and "would someone please meet us at Saco." Unknown to the Prechels, the weather awaiting them in the Saco area was anything but pleasant – the snow was 3 feet deep! A neighbor of the Kientzes, Charles "Holledge" Allen, remarked that Lizzie's folks had "picked the wrong time of the moon to come west to Montana." His prediction was 100 percent correct. Since there was no way to head off the relatives, the young couple simply had to make the best of a bad situation. Otto harnessed up his trusty team of horses to the sled and spent the entire day traveling to Saco. If that old sled could talk, it would tell its own story for it sits yet out on the homestead.

That night was spent in the town of Saco, resting up for the return trip north. Rain awakened the tired members of the party during the night. The following day it was a slow, tired group of travelers and two exhausted horses that finally reached the little home on the knoll. The rain had softened the once hard crust of the deep snow, causing the horses to sink down with every step they took. The Preschels stayed three weeks and then Otto was able to take them by wagon to meet the train at Saco.

The abundance of moisture was a mixed blessing that year. Otto called it "the year of the mosquito." The Frenchman Creek flooded twice; although this didn't reach the Kientz home which was on higher ground, it did cause much hardship for the Mark Wrights, who were flooded out both times. Their new Buick car was also caught in the flash flood in June. It left a foot of water in the house, forcing the family to move upstairs. The cats belonging to the Wrights came to a bad end – drowning beneath the house. Since it was impossible to drag them out, the resulting stench reminded everyone of their presence.

The flooding resulted in a tragedy when the deputy assessor by the name of Murphy drowned as he was attempting to cross the swollen Milk River. His body was recovered by dragging, which resulted in the drowning of a man who was assisting with the dragging operation. The assessor's briefcase with the papers intact was rescued from the flood water.

The winter of 1916 was very hard. The cattle from the Turkey Track Ranch in Canada drifted down looking for feed. Jansey Tieden took care of some which wandered into his place and many others went as far as the Milk River Bridge.

During the spring of 1916, Arthur Prechel, one of Lizzie's brothers, decided that he would look the country over for a suitable location. The Albert Pehlke place was for sale at that time

- Albert, being Gust Pehlke's brother. But Mother Prechel wrote a letter in German to her son stating that he should "come home and we will go to North Dakota, as it should be better there!!"

Mrs. Prechel obviously left her daughter's home with a bad impression of Montana. The Albert Pehlke homestead now belongs to the Milton Olsen family. For many years after, each time Arthur Prechel visited the Kientzes he was ribbed about rejecting Montana land.

The five pet sheep which the Kientzes had acquired were sheared in June and Otto carried the wool to his neighbors, the Wrights, who lived on the Frenchman; but when he came over the hills, he could see that everything was flooded for the second time. The Wrights raised sheep and handled the wool for Otto, but this time Otto sold it at Saco for about 14 cents a pound.

The surrounding land now was well settled with a family on every half section. This is a totally different situation from what it is now. There was an unwritten rule that anyone was welcome for a meal and a bed – with no questions asked. Lizzie tells about the time a stranger stopped at the house and said he would like to spend the night there. Lizzie replied that Otto wasn't home and that she would have to ask him first. The man replied in no uncertain terms that he was going to stay anyway! The family feels to this day that this stranger was a fugitive. He wasn't the only one which came to the Kientz door looking for lodging and a home-cooked meal. Some would tell tales and others remained silent about their affairs. This homestead became known as Last Chance, an appropriate name as it seemed to be a favorite stopping spot.

Seed oats had been purchased that spring from Tom Tollefson, a neighbor several miles to the west, and this was seeded after the wild oats were weeded out. This 100 pounds of oats produced 22 bushels an acre that fall. Otto also raised some wheat and flax which went 22 bushels to the acre. The Kientzes had various garden spots over the years, the best location being located near their dam – producing a 23-pound head of cabbage, as one good example. There's an existing picture of this mammoth vegetable, so no one can dispute that claim.

Leona, the first child of the Kientzes, was born on June 24, 1917, at the family home. The midwife at this particular time was Mrs. Pehlke, Gus Pehlke's mother from the west farming bench, later known as the Forks community. Three years later, Luella was born to Otto and Lizzie. This time it was a fast-flying stork as this baby arrived before the midwife did.

Part 5

The Kientz family now numbered four: Otto, Lizzie and their two lively daughters, blonde Leona, nicknamed "Toots," and the dark-haired Luella, who is known as "Babe." The members of this family were closely knit and have remained so over the years.

Luella, number two daughter, reminisced about her childhood out on the windswept prairie.

"Winter snows brought out the homemade sleds, scoop shovels or toboggan for sliding down the rocky hills. With my long tresses trailing behind and lying flat on the sled, I glided through a patch of cockle burrs, which extended beyond the snow's crest. It took Mother quite some time to patiently comb out the burrs, and still retain my long hairdo."

Pet skunks were among the curiosities found on the place. A large hollowed out log served as a den. Several coyotes and a bob cat were also called pets, but never petted. We knew in the end, these animals would be sacrificed for their pelts.

Long winter evenings were spent playing pinochle with the Ericksons, their neighbors southwest of the Kientz homestead. Transportation to the Ericksons farm was team and sled, walking or skiing. Carl Erickson was noted for his delicious bachelor's bread, which I well remember. A few musicians spent evenings, warbling the "Red River Valley" and picking on a guitar. There was Allen Marshall with his violin, and I think, a mandolin. Dad played a fiddle, Mama played the organ and us kids, the guitar and also the organ.

In our teen years, we got our start raising bum lambs – compliments of the Henry Barton ranch. We would have between 20 and 30. The baby lambs were taught to drink by holding a finger in a bucket of milk, after a few days, they'd be ready to drink out of a half-tire filled with milk.

As the fastest drinkers had their share, they'd be lifted over into another pen. In the daytime, we had to watch for coyotes and at night, the lambs were herded into the barn. Lambs, of all the creatures, are the most playful and like children, they weren't always ready for bed.

So, it was a game to see who would win on getting them all into the barn at once. The first lambs in would be ready to come out by the time the first ones reached the door – a couple of stiff-legged jumps by the leader and the whole band would be promenading across the yard again. . . . and so there were the fun times and the hard times. This family remembers both, in amazing detail.

Leona commented that, "The baby lambs were brought each day from the Bartons. We harnessed up our own team to a rig, went cross country over the hills and got as close to the Barton ranch as we could, then tied up the horses, went down and carried the lambs back up for the trip home."

Leona mentioned that it was no problem feeding the pet skunks as they enjoyed a variety such as milk, cherries, grass hoppers, potatoes or anything from the table as long as it didn't contain much salt. If there were mice or dead jackrabbits, this made the menu that much more enjoyable for the wild pets. It was a cute sight to see a skunk eat, as they hold their food in their paws just like a cub bear and they would lap up milk like a cat. These animals were all caught in traps and released into a box to be transported to the buildings.

There was never any annoying skunk odors, as these animals were handled gently, with care always taken to avoid startling them. Unbelievable as it may sound, Leona transported a skunk alive alongside her in a car for a distance of over 20 miles – without a mishap.

Otto remembered that the year 1928 was a fair year crop wise, but the following year and the thirties were most discouraging.

By this time, Otto's cattle had increased with the original milk cow producing a calf each year and a few calves bought from

Alfred Minke [of the] The First National Bank, located where the Big Dome Hotel stands, held a mortgage on some fine cows raised by Boner Zenor, who lived a mile from Charlie Haynes' farm, north of Saco. The banker at Saco was R. D. Sutherland, who had been raised by a banker, W. E. C. Ross in Blue Earth, Minnesota, the hometown of Otto and Lizzie Kientz. Sutherland asked Kientz if perhaps he would like to buy the mortgaged cows, and Otto replied that he didn't have the money. The banker said that he would let Otto have the cash, with no strings attached. The four cows turned out to be a good investment as they were in excellent condition - big and fat and were real rustlers. It was necessary actually to bring them in for feed when winter set in.

Another man from Blue Earth eventually migrated to Hinsdale and acquired a job at the local bank. This young man was Harry Abbott, a former mailman for Elmore, MN, 10 miles from Blue Earth. He was quite an athlete, who would run behind the mail wagon to get his exercise. In later years, he went west and was an insurance salesman.

Saco was a booming town, before the depression set in. It was impossible for the lumber railcars to meet the demand for seasoned lumber, so many people settled for the green. After the green lumber dried, gaps appeared in the buildings.

There were four grocery stores and later another one, The Kronschnabels. There had been three banks at Saco, but never more than two at one time. Now in 1973, there are none.

Each spring Otto assisted Henry Barton, a neighbor to the south, with his lambing operation. The Barton's brand was estimated at about 1,000 head. Otto's job was tending the shed in the daytime. This was difficult work, especially hard on the back, although enjoyable to one who likes sheep. The newborn lambs had to be taught to nurse and it was necessary to brand the new lambs and the ewe with identical numbers, which were painted on. Thus number 16 lamb belonged to the ewe which carried number 16 also. Jim Austin, uncle of Harry Austin Sr., also hired Otto for this lambing operation in the Whitewater community.

One spring while the women were alone at the Kientz home, the pail-fed calves were put out to pasture. It was discovered shortly after, that they all died from unknown causes. An almost identical situation occurred at the Jim Austin ranch while Otto was working there, but in that case it was milk cows which suddenly died. When Otto returned home, the family learned from him that the bad luck was caused by Death Camas. The family never lost any of their lambs from this fungi, because the girls went out early in the morning to gather the poisonous mushrooms which often appealed to the sheep.

A variety of berry bushes growing wild provided the family with jellies, juices and syrup for the table. Service berries, also commonly known as June berries, were a favorite. One year, Lizzie canned 100 quarts of these berries and still had extra raw ones to sell. Buffalo berries, another common wildberry, were gathered by beating the bushes with sticks, and allowing the crimson berries to fall onto tarps, which had been spread beneath the bushes. Picking these berries by hand would have been a slow, painful process, as there were thorns intermingled with the berries. These buffalo berries were gathered after the first frost, as the fruit is much sweeter then. The Buffalo berries produced a milky juice that resulted in a clear ruby red jelly. Chokecherries were also picked whenever they were available.

Lizzie's talent as a seamstress was much in demand in the neighborhood. The fabric was provided by the customer and then Lizzie designed a pattern to suit the particular individual. One customer was a hired man of Mark Wright's. Mrs. Kientz sewed two nifty shirts for him – both being silk, one in red and the other a bright green. The story got back to Kientzes that on a Saturday night, when this particular gentleman was all decked out in his new shirt, his horse bucked him off into Frenchman Creek. This unplanned baptism forced him to retrace his tracks and change clothes – this time donning his second silk shirt for the evening. The women in the Wright family were frequent customers of Lizzies. Another item which proved quite popular was the handmade neckties.

Machinery used during these years was all horse machinery – plow, disk, rake, mower and binder. All the homesteaders were supposed to prove up 40 acres within three years after filing on their homestead. Some broke up more land, but because of rocky conditions, Otto decided the rest should be left for grazing. Eventually some of this plowed land was put back into pasture.

After his own work was done, Otto assisted his good neighbor, Mark Wright, with dirt work which was done with four horses and a scraper – building dikes and ditches. There was also ice to be put up and wood sawed for fuel - "A pile as big as a straw stack," says Otto. Otto worked for 16 years for this neighbor. He also built fence – 6 miles in all, at $20 a mile. Bill Wodtkey, another Frenchman neighbor who was originally from Indiana, exchanged work with Otto at harvest time. Bill would then be free to help Otto with the fence building at Wrights. Wodtkey, incidentally, shared the same birthdate with Otto.

During one lunch break for the fence builders, two riders ventured up. One was a coyote trapper, Jim Hall, and a stranger dressed in an army uniform. Otto inquired about him from Hall and he answered that, "This is my 'nephew'," Otto said, while relating the incident that the stranger was no more his nephew than I was! You never could believe what Hall said – but he sure knew how to catch the coyotes! Jim Hall took the stranger, who was Henry Barton, far to the north of Genevieve community to locate a homestead. The two Barton boys were later born in a sod house on land which was eventually sold to Clair Duncan.

Part 6

What are the memories that warm the heart after the years have swept past? Is it not the simple things? . . . and so it is with the Kientz family.

Fifty years ago, the town of Shelby, Montana, was rolling out the red carpet in preparation for the World's Heavyweight Championship fight between Gibbons and Dempsey. The main road, which is the route of Highway 2 now, was experiencing muddy conditions, so the traffic was rerouted north. The sparsely-traveled Frenchman Creek Road became a bypass road for many travelers en route to the fight and the Kientz home overlooking this road became a "ringside seat."

Threshing machines or separators, as they were sometimes called, were a frequent sight since there was more and more cropland in the area. Otto was on many threshing crews and for several years managed entire outfits himself, such as Jess Miller's.

At this particular time, Otto's in-laws once again came to visit. John Tollefson, who owned a car, brought the Prechels out from Saco. Lizzie's dad was then hired by Mark Wright to pitch bundles. "He wasn't too old, about 70, and he worked like a good fellow," remarked Otto. In 1924, Otto ran George Mellen's threshing machine, "a big outfit, 36-inch cylinder." This rig was followed by a cook car borrowed from Mauchs, neighbors to the NE. This crew was fortunate enough to have their own cook, a lady by the name of Mrs. Goldman. The threshers started at the Saco flat where George Knudson Jr. now lives. Others in the area who hired the crew were Roggness, Breipohls, Fred Erickson and others. After finishing on the flat, they went north and crossed the river and threshed all along Frenchman Creek for various neighbors. Another time, Otto ran Martin Hanson's separator, going west in the Forks area, threshing for Otto Schleuner, Stan McNamara and Sam Gater, (nicknamed "Black Sam") only to mention a few.

It was this same year, 1924, but on another threshing crew that "Rattlesnake Olson," one of those men who had helped Otto locate on his homestead, met his death by falling off a loaded bundle wagon and being run over. This occurred on the Jim Whiteman place, now occupied by George Soennichsen.

After an absence of 13 years, Minnesota became the destination for a trip in June of 1926. This was a surprise venture, "We didn't tell anyone that we were coming and we didn't tell anyone we were going," said Otto. The family camped and picnicked along the way. With a tent which fitted over the car and which extended 6 feet away from the vehicle, everyone managed nicely. Otto and Lizzie slept outside the car, protected by the extended tent while the two little girls slept inside the car. This was a most practical arrangement, enabling the family to roll up bedding and tent and depart early in the morning while Leona and Luella slept undisturbed. Whenever their route took them anywhere close to a city, they managed to travel during the early morning hours, thus avoiding traffic. You can well imagine what a delight this was for the tousled-headed, sleepy country girls, peering from the Model T Ford car, trying their best to absorb every detail of the new sights along the way.

To those unfamiliar with a 1914 Model T car, it can be described as barely adequate, as there was no door on the driver's side, plus cloth curtains and eisenglass side windows. [Note: The material was celluloid, although people referred to it as Eisenglass.] Otto claims that you could tell the speed you were going by the amount of noise made by the flapping of the windows! The travelers experienced many flat tires during their trip and once, the connecting rod went out. A replacement was purchased right there at Worthington, MN and Otto put the rod in on the spot and they were soon ready to continue their trip.

In preparation for the trip, Otto had constructed a regular cupboard, which fit into the opening on the driver's side and which rested on the running board. The cupboard could be raised and served as a table in this position. This handy invention was also the storage cupboard for their food as they traveled. A toolbox, which was standard equipment for this type of automobile, also rested on one of the running boards.

This 1914 Model T Ford car had been originally owned by Otto's brother-in-law, his oldest sister's husband, who had traded it in on a Chevy. Walter Kientz, in turn, bought it for $100, drove it out here to Montana and resold it to Otto, also for $100. Years later this car was sold for $15 to a collector in Minnesota.

Strange as it may seem, some of the Minnesota relations gave the Kientz family a cool reception upon their arrival at Blue Earth, Minnesota. Not recognizing them, one person threatened them with a hoe and another said he would call the police when Otto insisted on camping there. Even the little girls receiving the brush-off when they would go up to the door of the relative and ask for cookies or maybe supper. It was all a practical joke, instigated by Otto with his grassroots humor, and still is amusing [to the] relations whenever they get together and reminisce how the Minnesotan relations didn't recognize their own blood relations from Montana. This vacation was an enjoyable and rare treat for the Kientzes, who had not been away from the state of their birth for 13 years, and for Leona and Luella, who had never met their relations before, with the exception of their maternal grandparents and an uncle.

There were 40 first cousins of Otto's on his dad's side, and almost as many of his mother's side. They, along with their offsprings, added up to quite a group. Lizzie had very few relatives except her immediate small family. Although Kientzes stayed six weeks away from Montana, it was virtually impossible to visit everyone. On their way back home, they stopped off at Tolley, North Dakota to visit Lizzie's youngest brother, Arthur Prechel, who was a bachelor at that time. Leona said she can still recall the taste of that delicious sausage which they had for breakfast at her uncle's home. During an outdoors band concert at Tolley, Otto spied a cousin who had lived in earlier years at Blue Earth, so this also was a pleasant surprise to once again renew this acquaintance.

When the Kientzes arrived back home to the prairie, they were greeted by a mother hen and several new offsprings, which had hatched during their absence, much to the amusement of the two girls. The Whitbreds had done the chicken chores during their absence of six weeks.

Neighborliness was at an all-time high during these early years. The homesteaders assisted one another with different types of chores such as butchering, putting up ice, etc. One winter day the Hess children, Maud, who is Mrs. Ernest Erickson, Mary, who was the late Mrs. Herman Knuth, and their brother, Cecil, skied over to their neighbors to the north. Tied onto their skies was a package of pork – a "thank you" to Otto for helping with the butchering of a hog.

The midnight ride of Paul Revere seems like children's play in comparison to an errand of mercy made by Otto upon the request of a neighbor. An elderly neighbor, Mrs. Andrew Hjort, had passed away one night and so Otto bundled up, saddled up a horse and rode into Saco, the distance of 23 miles – this wasn't April weather as Paul Revere enjoyed during his famous ride – but this was in the fierce cold of December to deliver the message to the A. J. Erickson family, as some of the Ericksons had moved to Saco for the winter. Mrs. Erickson was the daughter of the deceased, Mrs. Hjort. Otto said he could hear Mrs. Erickson cry over the loss of her mother during the night. Otto shared a bed with Harold Erickson until the next morning. Consider the fact that the Kientz family had no way of knowing if Otto had reached Saco safely or was lying somewhere frozen to death in the subzero temperature.

In these days, it was taken for granted that a physician would travel to his needy patients, regardless of the miles involved. Once Dr. Minnick, living at Saco, was called to deliver a baby on the east side of the Frenchman. The central operator, for the Mutual Telephone Company, Mrs. Herman Knuth on Turkey Track, was not at home, so Jansey Tieden, who understood the workings of the phone system, manipulated the wires for this emergency and was able to reach Dr. Minnick and ask him to come out north to the home of Walter Kientz. In due time, Dr. Minnick arrived and was met by the expectant father. They rode double on horseback across the raging spring water at Frenchman Creek, but by the time they reached the home, the baby had been born. Lizzie, sister-in-law of the new mother, had everything nicely under control so Dr. Minnick took a nap before he returned to Saco. A typical day in the life of a rural doctor.

Part 7

The depression days have been appropriately named, the "Dirty Thirties" - dust storms often times obscuring the very sun in the sky – fierce winds blowing the thistles against the barbed wire fences, which in turn caught much of the moving topsoil which had quite possibly traveled for many miles before coming to rest in the form of gray banks of dust. There have been drier years since, but none took the toll as did these discouraging years endured by the homesteaders in the '30s. Summer fallowing, mostly on an experimental basis, was just beginning to appear, but most conservation practices, so common place now, were simply unheard of then on the Montana prairie.

The homesteaders' grain crops in these days of drought, amounted to practically nothing – but each year, spring seeding was done with hope and a prayer that "this year will be better."

Many were the times that the Kientzes didn't as much as get their seed back in the fall.

As if the weather wasn't hardship enough for these struggling people, there was also the scourge of grasshoppers. Clouds of them blotting out the sun – ready to devour anything green. Lizzie tried in vain to protect her cabbage plants from the hungry insects by placing screens over them, but the hoppers eventually won out by managing to crawl under the screens. These pesky insects did provide juicy morsels and also a diversion for the chickens, which didn't have too much to eat anyway. But this unusual chicken feed rendered the chicken flesh inedible. Eventually, the application of grasshopper poison came to the aid of the settlers. The poisoned bran was devoured by the "hoppers" and did prove effective in eradicating them.

Perhaps mention should be made of the closure of the area's banks. There was no advance warning – one day a depositor had money in the bank and the next day there was none. The larger depositors did get a bit of back interest, but it didn't amount to much. Otto recalls that his wouldn't have bought a meal, so he told them to keep it. Apparently the banks had lent out too much money over the years without receiving good security. Security was generally in the form of land, which at that time was worth very little. Katherine Arson, across Frenchman Creek, had proved up on her homestead and, desiring to sell it, accepted a check for $500. She kept it a day or two and then took it to the Hinsdale

Bank where she was told that the bank wouldn't honor it. Her land was no longer hers and she was out the $500.

The pinch of the depression was felt in many different ways. Otto and his daughter, Leona, tell about the time that Otto assisted Mark Wright in trailing his cows into Saco. When the town came into view, Mark rode ahead to see about the cattle railcars which he had ordered. He found out that his trip had been for nothing as the railroad cars were not in town and no one at the depot knew when they could be expected. Discouraged, the men started trailing the cattle back toward the north country, selling the cattle along the way for $15 a head to whoever had the money – Joe Mavencamp and Lochiel Edward's were two of the buyers. These shorthorn cows were big and in their prime – Otto says he helped butcher one which weighed 1,200 pounds. This was a sample of the quality beef raised during those years by Mark Wright on his Frenchman Creek ranch.

Strange as it may seem to young cattlemen of this day and age, Russian thistles were utilized for cattle feed during the depression winters. Otto and the other livestock owners who were in "the same boat," raked up the thistles while they were still green and juicy and stacked them – the stacks settled gradually and as Otto with his usual wit, so aptly described it, "We dished the thistles out just like pancakes!" This handy feed certainly must have been provided by the Almighty, as the cattle found this unusual, monotonous sounding diet much to their liking, thus saving them from possible starvation and their owner from more hardship.

One spring, Otto decided to run for the position of trustee on the Tollefson School Board. His opponent that particular year was Art Eklund, the father of Mrs. Charlie Hayes. It was the usual bad weather on the first Saturday of April, but never-the-less, every eligible voter cast their ballot in this hot election. Perhaps the statement of Mark Right's to the effect that "Otto deserves the position, as he has always kept up the road to the school," swayed a few voters, but anyway, Otto won over his opponent by three or four votes. This school district was rather vast and included even the Stuart Brookie across the Frenchman. Otto and the clerk of the school board, Mr. Whitbread, visited that household on one occasion to check on the home tutoring being done by Mrs. Brookie for her daughter, Lois, Mrs. Willard Bowman.

Anne Poland Dippy, who had come from Ellen-burg, Washington, to teach at the Tollefson School, recalls that her salary was $65 a month. She boarded at the Kientz home for $15 per month with transportation to and from school "thrown in with the deal." A few of the teachers at this school, which incidentally closed in the mid-40s, were Bernadine Brandt Smith, native of Whitewater; Ruth Kappel Dull, living at Saco, and the late Bonnie O'Brien Ivanovitch, who lived for many years in the north Whitewater area. The late Mrs. Ed Erickson also taught at this school. The average attendance was from 10 to 15 pupils.

By this time the water situation on the Kientz homestead had been solved with a good well dug close by, after years of hauling water. The prairie had become pock-marked by attempts at locating the elusive water vein. Tests were done with an auger, sometimes water was found but joy was short-lived as it turned out to be alkali. It was figured out that a total of 1,000 feet had been dug altogether in the water searching attempts. The 53-foot present well was dug in 1929, [and] handmade drill and post hole auger were the well drilling tools used. Neighbor Carl Erickson helped install the casing which had been purchased from Henry Math of Whitewater.

The government-sponsored WPA program was a financial shot in the arm for the needy families in those depressing days of the 30s. Jansey Tieden, who became associated with the WPA in Phillips County, offered Otto a foreman's or "pushers job." The policy was two weeks of employment then two weeks off in order that more men could be involved. Various types of labor were done, such as fencing, building dams on government land, poisoning gophers; traveling from the Canadian line to the Little Rockies south of Malta. Otto had a different crew each time he went out on the two-week stretches. The government provided tents, even large ones for the horses. Otto Busche and Bill Gust of the Forks community to the West, were two of the cooks. Some former WPA workers remembered were Harry Brown, Archie Ulness, Fred and Jerome Allery, Westley Wright, Otto Schleusner and Oliver Tollefson. At one time, Otto worked at the Legion

Health Plunge, now known as the Sleeping Buffalo Recreation Area, and he used tools belonging to Paul Daellenbach of Malta, who was the foreman on that job.

The women at home kept quite busy with chores while Otto was gone during the WPA years. Lizzie kept her eye on the trap line, which they had set on their own land; sometimes finding it necessary to shoot a badger which was unlucky enough to get caught and also shooting coyotes. She always managed to be available when a helping hand was needed, driving a one-horse buggy on errands, raking and stacking hay and even hauling the sacked grain into Saco - Otto taking one wagon and team ahead while Lizzie followed behind. Mishaps during these jaunts makes one think that the horses were actually daring Lizzie to handle them. On one occasion this couple enjoyed a spectacle of brilliant shooting stars in the sky – Otto remarked that this was a sight that they have never seen since.

Saturday night dances every two weeks at the Valleytown schoolhouse to the East relieved the tedium of the work-filled days. The Kientz family, with their multi-talents, was the core of the musical group – Babe and Toots played guitars, Lizzie the organ and Otto on the fiddle, providing a lively time for the neighbors and friends attending. The Kappel sisters lent their voices to the occasions and Walt Hoyer, who in later years became the Malta police officer, sometimes brought his fiddle, singing one of his favorites, "When the Moon Comes Over the Mountain."

Fiddling required more than ordinary effort for this man, as he had a stub hand, but he managed somehow with a special strap. The hat was passed around during the evening and although the compensation was small, it was appreciated. The music played until the sun came up and when the family arrived home, the cows were milked and the sheep fed before the Kientzes retired to bed.

On Sunday, the church organist didn't show up for Lutheran services so the preacher, with a twinkle in his eye, asked Otto if perhaps he had brought his fiddle along. Otto says, "The preacher knew full well that I'd been out all night playing for a dance!" The dances at Valleytown had to eventually close down because of an invasion of bootleggers, spoiling the good times for these hard-working people in the area.

Part 8

Certainly, no people lived closer to God and nature than the early-day farmers who tilled the land and ranchers who tended the livestock. The Kientz family did their part with constant toil and sweat of the brow – Mother Nature did what remained to be done, for better or worse.

This partnership of man and nature resulted in large prolific gardens on this homestead – the Kientz family were always alert to opportunities and this one was ideal. The gumbo surrounding the little home on the cobblestone hill was rich soil. It was an excellent site for the raising of vegetables which provided a variety for the family larder. The Saco food stores benefited by these lush gardens besides the many individual customers who were delighted to find such a handy supply of cabbage for sauerkraut and other good vegetables – beets, tomatoes, cucumbers, carrots, rutabagas, onions, peas and beans - all in abundance when the weather cooperated. Mention was made of the time that rutabagas were rolled into the family cellar on a sloping board and this storage place was filled so full that it was impossible to enter. Ground cherries or husk tomatoes as they are sometimes referred to, were a very popular item. Leona said her mother spent many hours picking these off the low-growing bushes. The ground cherries were not only tasty eaten raw, but made mouth-watering pies – these were made much in the manner of apple pie. This unusual fruit was sold fresh and also canned. Peanuts were grown as a novelty one year and after they were dug and toasted, "they didn't taste too bad at all," remarked Leona. Whenever a local store ran low on vegetables, a card was sent by mail to Otto, mentioning what was needed and the quantity. So the Model T Ford was loaded to the brim with the vegetables and delivered to C. P. Martin, the local grocer, or whoever wished to purchase the vegetables. Mr. Martin remarked one time to Otto, "Well, I might just as well turn the store over to you, you own half of it anyway!"

On a good year the family could accumulate a total of $20 from produce, including butter and eggs, which they sold in the store. It was always an easy task to sell these items – the vegetables usually sold for five to six cents per pound.

Pictures in the Kientz family album attest to the bountiful gardens which were Lizzie's pride and joy. She dearly loved to work among the vegetable plants. Pea picking and haying always came at the same time – when Lizzie was done stacking hay, she would start on the peas, which were placed on screens to dry in the sunlight. Peas were picked by the dishpan full, so the combination of these two jobs meant long days even for a woman as full of vitality as Lizzie Kientz. Pressure canning had not come into its own, so beans were kept by pouring hot vinegar over them in the jars which were tightly sealed.

Windbreaks were a must for these people residing on the open prairies where the winds had no mercy. A.J. Erickson grew a variety of bushes and trees so seeds were available when Otto was ready to start the rows of trees, which would be planted on the edge of the garden site. Maple seeds had been planted to no avail, as the harsh Montana climate was not suited for this Minnesota tree. It was discovered that caraganas did quite well under local conditions, so these seeds were planted. The green borders added a welcome touch of green to the bleak landscape. The trees grew so well and took so much moisture that a different garden site had to be selected.

Part 9

Diamond willows brought from Frenchman Creek have played a unique role in the lifetime of Otto Kientz, providing him with a handy supply of slender but sturdy fence posts. Sixty years is an unbelievably long life for a post supporting several strands of barbed wire and holding up under the stress of cattle rubbing, exposure to the elements, the weight of snow banks and accumulations of Russian thistles caught in the barbs of the fence. But these locally grown willow posts are still solidly supporting the fence surrounding the Kientz fields and pastures, a sort of symbol you might say to the steadfastness of these homesteaders.

Not only did the diamond willow have practical uses, but Otto with his many hours of hand work, has brought forth a hidden beauty and consequently developed his own particular style of handcrafted tables, lamps, candleholders, canes and footstools.

One hatrack was constructed and adorns the office of County Attorney Willis McKeon at Malta – much to the pleasure of clients who usually placed their hats on the floor. The rugged shaped diamond designs finally exposed and highlighted by all this whittling, sanding and varnishing lend their special beauty to these various works of art. The word, handcrafts, is electricity on the Kientz farm. Every single tool is hand driven. Imagine the time and accuracy which is involved in just one phase of lamp making – boring a center hole down the length of a diamond willow. It requires steady hands, a keen eye and obviously, the patience of Job.

Otto branched out, if you will pardon the pun, into another type of woodworking and that is working with cedar. Unlike the willow, cedar must be obtained from quite a distance away. Certain areas around Ft. Peck Reservoir for instance, nearly 70 miles to the SE have old fragrant cedar trees lying dead and forgotten by men who engineered the construction of Ft. Peck Dam in the 1930s.

The cedar roots have such fantastic shapes that they would have to be classified as modern art. These finished products have to be seen to be fully appreciated. It takes an eye as perceptive as Otto's to recognize a drab, broken, uprooted tree lying in a deep ravine, as a potential "diamond in the rough."

These gleaming originals sell like hotcakes – and without a sales pitch. This time-consuming hobby provided a satisfying pastime for Otto, particularly during the long, cold winter months. There are Otto's handcrafted items in Japan, Norway, Canada and many different states, mailed by purchasers to friends and relatives living in these far-away places. Word-of-mouth and proud display by the numerous purchases are the only forms of advertising.

Rug weaving in a separate building filled many hours for this creative family. The cotton warp used is either red or green and is ordered from Sears Roebuck mail order house. This is the only item which had to be purchased for the rug weaving process. The rag strips were torn from discarded clothing or else were remnants, courtesy of drapery and upholstery shops. Leona declared that worn overalls make the best rugs. Three miles of solid rug have been woven since Otto built the loom in 1936 – carrying the plans in his personal memory bank since he viewed his sister's loom back in Minnesota in the year 1926. This handmade loom was a remarkable piece of ingenuity. Besides the wooden frame, you see a metal drive from a windshield of a Model T. five connecting rods, wire hammers from netting fence, door springs, rubber inner tubes, roller from an old binder, copper wire from generators and the most unbelievable items of all – "eyelets from mama's corset."

This all put together produces the tightest woven rag rugs available. Credit must also go to Leona, who operates the loom. Not only are these rugs durable and completely washable, each one is very beautiful with borders of solid colors on each end framed with red and green fringes - a tribute to the chief color coordinator, Lizzie. Even when she was bedridden, Lizzie personally chose the particular color combination for each individual rug. No two rugs are alike unless specifically ordered by customers. These rugs also found their way to foreign countries and other states. Many are found among shower gifts and also are given by the Kientz family as gifts on the occasion of open house for a neighbor. These rugs can never be confused with the commercial loosely woven rugs commonly found on store shelves – the beautiful designs and quality workmanship are the Kientz trademark.

When Otto was asked who prompted him to build a loom, he replied, "We were simply all tired of braiding rugs."

Part 10

A multitude of preparatory steps went into a typical washday in the homesteader's modest home. It's a certainty that the modern-day housewife would think twice before swapping places with the housewives of the early 1900s in rural Montana. Doing the family laundry was considered almost an art. First, the water was pumped at the well and hauled by a horse-drawn wagon, and then the cold water was heated on the kitchen stove – the same stove which heated the house and cooked the meals. There hasn't been a central heating system built since, that performed as many tasks as did this stove, still used and treasured in the Kientz home.

The laundry soap, which was made by Lizzie from scraps of tallow saved for this purpose, along with water and lye, was also cooked on the stove. The mixture was cooked and stirred to a thick consistency and checked frequently with Lizzie's thermometer. If the proper temperature wasn't adhered to, the result was a crumbly soap instead of the hard, long-lasting bars preferred by the women of that era. This hot, smelly mixture was then poured into a wooden box which had been lined with a cloth. A knife was used to cut the yellow soap into bars just before it was completely set.

The back-weakening task of washing clothes was done on a rigid metal, wooden-framed washboard, which was propped on its two legs at an angle in the washtub. The soapy clothes were rubbed, turned, dipped into the wash water until sufficiently clean. The rinsing was done in tubs of clear water and the next step, that of wringing the excess water out of the clothes, was accomplished by putting them through the wringer attached to the side of the tub. Otto was called on the scene to man the wringer whenever his heavy underwear was put through. No rubber or plastic gloves were available to protect the hands from this harsh work.

The clothes were hung to dry on the clotheslines a few steps west of the house, regardless of the weather. Leona recalls the fragrance of the freshly laundered clothes, permeating the house on these weekly washdays.

Flour sacks were boiled in the copper wash boiler to aid in the removal of the printed advertising. A bit of lye was added to the simmering water as these were the days before bleach and such laundry aids. After this boiling period, the hot, steamy flour sacks were dipped out with a long wooden spoon and then were scrubbed white on the washboard. This might seem like a lot of bother for just cloth sacks, but these large sacks served for dish towels, quilt backings and various other practical purposes in every household – the uses were limited only by the housewife's imagination.

Ironing clothes was done with heavy flatirons, which were heated on the wood-burning stove. If the iron passed the spit test, it was ready for wood action; the detachable wooden handles were clamped on the top of the hot iron and the work began. There was always a spare iron waiting on the stove when the first iron cooled off.

Quilt making was still another activity for the women. A wooden quilt frame constructed by Otto was used to hold the quilt taut while busy fingers sewed the yarn or string at regular intervals over the quilt.

The yarn was tied in little tufts holding the backing, batting and cover together in sandwich fashion. These quilt tops were made from blocks of various scraps of fabrics sewn together producing a rainbow of colors to dress up a bed and which kept the occupant cozy during the bitter cold Montana winter.

A never-ending variety of tasks seemed to run bumper-to-bumper for men and women alike – but busy-ness is happiness.

Lizzie's delectable cooking was the talk of the community. One special dish which delighted the family can't go unmentioned, and that was roast sagehen. The pieces were first browned after receiving a generous coating of flour and seasoning, then placed into a baking dish. Milk was poured over and then it cooked slowly for hours in the oven. The combination meat and cream gravy was a gourmet dish and always impressed any guest who was lucky enough to eat at the Kientz home on that particular day.

A serenity seems to prevail over this quaint country home. No welcome mat lies at the door, nor is it necessary. An intangible something envelopes you as you step across the threshold and somehow you are no longer a stranger to the kindly personalities abiding here.

Sometimes there's a story of uncommon people which literally begs to be told. The one which concerned the joys and heartaches of a unique family living on the prairie land of northeastern Montana, where the land is forever bleak and the climate extreme.

Epilogue

By 1980, Leona and Otto had moved to Malta, MT. Many homesteaders who moved to town, would also have their house moved as well. This was not the case with the Kientzes, as the walls of their original home were insulated with sand and could not be moved. The structure still stands to this day.

While their home in Malta did have modern amenities, Leona and her father continued to make and sell their handcrafts. Their rag rugs were particularly popular. Leona continued the rug making even after her father's death on March 25, 1984.

Leulla "Babe" the eldest daughter of Otto and Lizzie, married Arnold Loftus and moved to Bremerton WA decades prior to the publication of the Kientz interviews. She passed away March 10, 1999.

Leona "Toots" Kientz died Oct 2, 2014 at the age of 97.

About The Author

Helen (Welch) DePuydt was born of an immigrant mother and Oklahoma born father and raised on a homestead in Northeastern Montana. Helen journaled throughout her childhood and her first published writing started with a writing contest which won her the First Prize of $50. Since then, Helen has authored a multitude of short stories most of which are her own memories of her life and the homestead life of her mother and other residents of the state of Montana. Her writings have been published in local, state, and national newspapers and magazines including: The Phillips Country News, The Glasgow Courier, and the Montana Magazine.

Other titles by author Helen DePuydt:

Montana Memories

Available through Amazon.com

About The Publisher

ReesaBird Studios is an art, illustration, design service owned and operated by Theresa (DePuydt) Johnson. Theresa was born in Northeastern Montana, the youngest of ten children. Theresa began drawing at an early age and had her first published illustration featured in *Hilights* magazine at the age of 8. In 1994, she earned a Bachelor of Fine Arts degree with emphasis in Graphic Design from Montana State University and has since worked as a freelance artist-illustrator in the Portland, OR and Vancouver, WA area. Theresa Johnson is the illustrator of the popular children's books *Rojo The Perfectly Imperfect Llama, Rojo Where's My Hair,* and *The Kite That Touched The Sky.*

For more information about Theresa's illustration services:

artist.theresa.johnson@gmail.com

www.theresajohnson.com

instagram.com/theresaartist

instagram.com/artist.theresa.johnson/

facebook.com/artbytheresajohnson/

Made in the USA
Middletown, DE
19 February 2022

61552338R00050